Reproducibles, Activities, And Ideas To Develop

Critical Thinking

For the Middle and Upper Grades

by Laurie Rozakis

SCHOLASTIC
PROFESSIONAL BOOKS

New York • Toronto • London • Auckland • Sydney

With love and thanks, I dedicate
this book to all the fine teachers
who have enriched my life:
Barbara Bengels, Chris LaRosa,
Ed Leigh, Jack McGrath,
Jim Pepperman, Jennifer Richmond,
Elizabeth Simmons, Lenore Strober,
and Tom Thibadeau.

Designed by Nancy Metcalf
Production by Intergraphics
Cover design by Vincent Ceci
Cover art by Beth Glick
Illustrations by Shelley Austin, Joe Chicko, and Terri Chicko

ISBN 0-590-49157-1

Contents

Introduction

Critical thinking skills are essential. Today's students will inherit a complex and rapidly changing world, a world in which they'll be required to absorb new ideas, examine and interpret information, apply knowledge, and solve unconventional problems. To do that effectively, they'll need to develop systematic ways of thinking and reasoning. In short, they'll need to think about their thinking. The good news? Thinking skills *can* be taught—if you work toward creating a classroom environment that encourages initiative, independence, and originality.

This book is designed to help you do just that. On the pages that follow, you'll find dozens of strategies for helping your students reflect on their own thinking processes and to become more active and successful learners. The strategies are organized according to a hierarchy of critical thinking skills, beginning with the skills of recognition and recall, and working up to the more advanced skills of analysis and synthesis. Using some or all of the following steps with each activity will help students to think about what they are doing and how they are doing it.

1. Read each activity aloud or have a student read it.
2. Ask the students questions to encourage and assess their understanding of the problem.
3. Solicit possible strategies for finding a solution.
4. Observe and question what the students are doing.
5. Give helpful hints to those students who seem to be having difficulty.
6. Point out the trickiest parts of the problem.
7. Encourage students to relate the problem to others they've already solved.
8. Urge students to check their work and the reasoning behind it.
9. Discuss the solutions that individual students reach.
10. Encourage students to identify the various strategies they use to solve the problem.

Be sure to leave plenty of time for students to reflect on their thinking before they dig into a problem, while they're working through it, and after they've solved it. Allowing time for reflection after an activity gives kids a chance to evaluate their problem-solving strategies and consider how they might adjust those strategies the next time around.

Finally, try to model critical thinking for your students by welcoming your own preconceptions and accepting unusual or unexpected strategies and solutions. Above all, encourage your students to think of themselves as thinkers.

Recognizing and Recalling

Before students can solve a problem, they need to understand it. And that means recognizing the facts associated with it and drawing on prior knowledge to recall related information that can be useful in working out a solution. The activities that follow will help improve your students' abilities to recognize facts and recall relevant information.

Each of these activities is designed to function as a complete lesson. You may want to use one in the morning to introduce the day's lessons, or as an end-of-day wrap-up. And bear in mind that many of these activities are suited to use in the content areas as well. For example, "Trivia Trackdown" (page 12) works especially well with science and social studies, while "Who Am I?" (page 17) fits any novel, short story, play, or narrative poem in your language arts curriculum.

Mystery Guest

This critical thinking activity will help students recognize and recall information. Before the class begins, write on slips of paper the names of well-known movie and television stars, sports figures, historical personages, comic strip or book characters, public figures, and so forth. Examples: Superman, Clara Barton, Santa Claus, Martin Luther King, Jr., the Earl of Sandwich, Madonna, Dick Tracy, Frankenstein, and Winnie the Pooh. Place all the slips of paper in a box, hat, or bowl.

Explain to students that in this activity they will have to identify the Mystery Guest by asking questions that can be answered with a yes or a no. Have a volunteer select a slip of paper, read the name to him- or herself, and pretend to be the person. Give the student a few minutes to prepare. At the same time, have the rest of the class make up a series of yes and no questions to ask the Mystery Guest. The person who correctly identifies the Mystery Guest gets to pick the next slip of paper.

Time Capsule

Here's a unique way to use literature to help your students recognize and gather key ideas. Begin by selecting a novel or short story that the entire class has read fairly recently. Write the title and the name of the main character on the chalkboard. Then ask students to list six to ten items from the book or story that were important to the main character. This can be done individually or in small groups. If the students read Gary Paulsen's *Hatchet,* for example, the list might look like this:

the hatchet	the bowandarrow
the airplane	the cave
fire	the lake
fish	the emergency
the raspberries	transmitter

Next, ask the class to put themselves in the main character's place. As the main character, which of these items might they want to save in a time capsule? What other items might they add? Have each student create a short list of things they would put in a time capsule for the main character, explaining why he or she chose each item.

You can expand this activity by having students make real time capsules for characters in other books and stories or for themselves. What items might best express other character's personalities—or their own? What items best capture the fictional or real experience? You might want to create a class time capsule. Ask each student to contribute one item. Then bury it somewhere on school grounds.

Rhyme and Reason

Play this rhyming game to help students build memory skills. Begin by choosing one word from the list below and announcing it to the class. Challenge the first child to state as many words as he or she can think of that rhyme with it. When that child becomes stumped, proceed to the second child, challenging him or her to think of more words. When the second child becomes stumped, proceed to the third child and so on. When a child repeats a previously used rhyming word, it's time to give the next child a fresh word. Award students a point for each word they can think of. Tally each child's score on the chalkboard. At the game's end, the student with the most points wins—and all the students have honed their critical thinking skills!

Word List

lamp	tame	bear
fright	take	beet
red	top	lap
tall	face	slide
lip	say	fade
bin	cat	chill

Turnabout Is Fair Play!

To help students with the important critical thinking skill of recalling, have them make up their own test questions for a piece of literature. To begin, arrange students into pairs. Explain that they are going to make up a test for a reading selection they have just completed. Explore with students the purpose of a test: to assess one's ability to recall important information. Tell students that their job now is to locate all the important information in the reading and make up questions that test whether others can remember the same important facts.

Then direct each pair to highlight all the key ideas in the story. From these key ideas, have students formulate test questions. These can take the form of true/false, multiple choice, fill-in-the-blank, or essay questions. Finally, compile all the questions and administer the test. Later discuss all the questions and the information students asked their classmates to recall.

Trivia Trackdown

Trivia Trackdown is a great way to sharpen two important critical thinking skills: recognizing and recalling. Have students create their own trivia questions based on literature the entire class has read or have them research general information on topics such as science, art, music, literature, sports, geography, movies, television, or history. Have students write their questions and answers on index cards, one question per card. Collect the cards and divide the class into two teams. Have the teams line up on opposite sides of the room. Ask Team A the first question. Continue down the line until a team member misses an answer. Have that student sit down, then begin asking questions of Team B. Alternate sides until only one person remains. Crown that person the Monarch of Trivia! On the following page are twenty trivia questions to start you off.

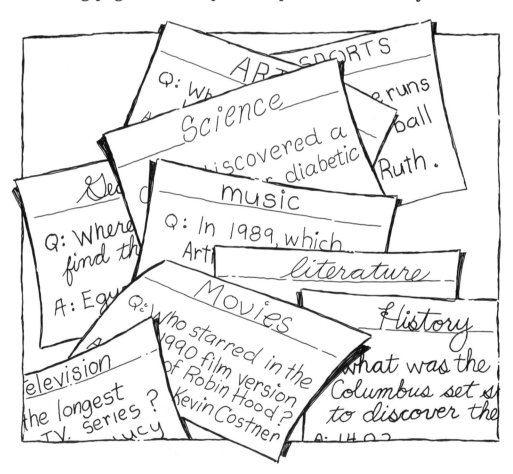

Trivia Trackdown
(cont.)

1. How many squares are there on a checkerboard?

2. What is the name of Mickey Mouse's dog?

3. What kind of animal is Babar?

4. What was the name of the Wright Brothers' airplane?

5. What is the capital of New York?

6. What do frogs have in their mouths that toads don't?

7. What is the name of the first woman to sit on the Supreme Court?

8. What's the most common bird on earth?

9. Who created *The Cat in the Hat?*

10. How many queen bees are in each hive?

11. Who was the second president of the United States?

12. How many teaspoons make up a tablespoon?

13. What two states share Kansas City?

14. Who is the Friendly Ghost?

15. Name the Great Lakes.

16. Who painted the *Mona Lisa?*

17. What substance inside corn makes it pop?

18. How many sides are there on a snowflake?

19. How many wings does a bee have?

20. How many pints are in a quart?

Recycled Words 1

RECYCLE BIN

Words can be recycled too! You can use the same word to make a lot of different words and phrases. The word *ice,* for example, can be used to make the word *icebox* or the phrase *ice water.*

Complete each of these words or phrases by writing in the same word in the spaces provided following each numeral.

Example: __coat__ check   __coat__ room   __coat__ of arms

1. _____ lash   _____ brow   _____ sight

2. _____ mark   _____ mine   _____ scape

3. _____ born   _____ England   _____ Year's Day

4. _____ work   _____ test   _____ block

5. _____ around   _____ away   _____ off

6. _____ shape   _____ wreck   _____ yard

7. _____ bow   _____ coat   _____ dance

8. _____ storm   _____ plow   _____ shoe

9. _____ pen   _____ house   _____ room

10. _____ roll   _____ shell   _____ nog

Name _____

Recycled Words 2

In Recycled Words 1, you saw that you can use the same word to make lots of different words and phrases. In that activity, you placed the recycled word first. Here, the recycled word may come *before* or *after* the blank.

Example: grape _fruit_   _fruit_ pie   _fruit_ cake

1. _____ fly   soda _____   _____ up

2. _____ boat   _____ keeper   doll _____

3. fat _____   _____ burglar   _____ call

4. fire _____   _____ kick   _____ card

5. lucky _____   _____ dust   _____ fish

6. _____ out   _____ eye   pitch _____

7. _____ color   _____ bug   white _____

8. _____ window   _____ signal   wind _____

9. straight _____   _____ drive   _____ up

10. front _____   _____ bell   _____ prize

WordPlay

Imagine you live in a world with only twenty words.
You can use these twenty words as much as you want,
but you cannot use any other words at all. In the
space below, list the twenty words you'd pick:

1. _____
2. _____
3. _____
4. _____
5. _____
6. _____
7. _____
8. _____
9. _____
10. _____

11. _____
12. _____
13. _____
14. _____
15. _____
16. _____
17. _____
18. _____
19. _____
20. _____

Now, write a paragraph using *only* your twenty words! Make sure your
paragraph has at least five sentences.

_____
_____
_____
_____
_____
_____
_____
_____
_____
_____

Who Am I?

Select any character from a book that you have read. Think about what you know about the character. Then complete this word web to describe the character as completely as you can:

How the character acts:

1. _____
2. _____
3. _____
4. _____

How the character feels:

1. _____
2. _____
3. _____
4. _____

Character's name:

_____

How the character looks:

1. _____
2. _____
3. _____
4. _____

What the character says:

1. _____
2. _____
3. _____
4. _____

Help Is on the Way

Imagine that you are a character in a book, short story, or poem that you have read. Write a letter to an advice columnist, mentioning all your problems.

_____

_____

_____

_____

_____

_____

_____

_____

_____

_____

Now, acting as the advice columnist, answer the letter. Suggest possible ways for the character to solve his or her problems.

_____

_____

_____

_____

_____

_____

_____

_____

_____

_____

What's My Letter? 1

Below is a list of definitions for words that begin with the letter H. See how many you can guess.

Words that Start with H

1. Balls of ice that fall from the sky _____

2. A 17-syllable Japanese poem _____

3. Not whole _____

4. A patty of chopped beef _____

5. An allergy to grasses and weeds _____

6. The organ that pumps blood _____

7. A great person, who people admire _____

8. Not low _____

9. The study of past events _____

10. A country known for tulips _____

What's My Letter? 2

Below is a list of definitions for words that begin with the letter L. See how many you can guess.

Words that Start with L

1. An object that provides light   _____

2. Very big   _____

3. A sound of delight   _____

4. Not willing to work; inactive   _____

5. The opposite of right   _____

6. To depart   _____

7. A sour yellow fruit   _____

8. A wild, spotted catlike animal   _____

9. Where you go to borrow books   _____

10. The opposite of big   _____

Mind Squeeze

Take two minutes to look at the words and objects on this page. Then turn the page over and see how many you can recall. Good luck!

HOMEWORK

SUMMER VACATION

SUNGLASSES

LUNCH

STUDY!

RAINBOW

GOOD!

Name _____

Soup's On!

It's dinner time, but what shall you eat? Complete this page to help you think of a menu.

Food that begins with b:

1. _____
2. _____
3. _____
4. _____
5. _____

Fast food:

1. _____
2. _____
3. _____
4. _____
5. _____

Food that is white: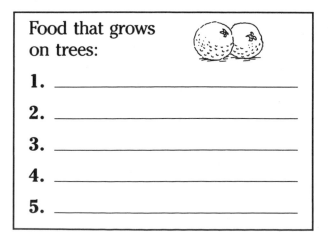

1. _____
2. _____
3. _____
4. _____
5. _____

Food that grows below ground: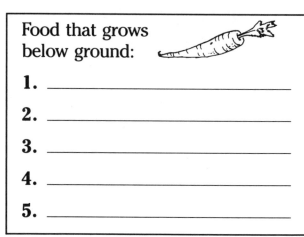

1. _____
2. _____
3. _____
4. _____
5. _____

Food that grows on trees:

1. _____
2. _____
3. _____
4. _____
5. _____

Now, list your five favorite foods:

1. _____
2. _____
3. _____
4. _____
5. _____

Distinguishing and Visualizing

People who think critically are adept at distinguishing between relevant and irrelevant details and at visualizing strategies and procedures that will help them solve a problem. By distinguishing and visualizing, children can solve problems in more logical, systematic, and efficient ways. The activities in this section will guide students through developing these skills.

Research shows that students who work in small groups of two to four children each tend to solve more problems. So you might want to try a collaborative approach to these activities. "Origami" (page 24), "Set the Scene" (page 26), and "Stargazing" (page 31) are particularly well suited to group work.

Origami

A great way to build visualization skills is by introducing your students to the Japanese art of paper-folding—origami.

Give your students these step-by-step instructions for creating a folded-paper rabbit:

1. Fold square in half vertically (GH). Unfold. Fold in half horizontally (EF) and unfold. Fold point A to point D, creating diagonal CB. Unfold and fold point B to point C, making the diagonal AD. Unfold. These four folds are "helping" folds, made to crease the paper so that subsequent folds will be easier.
2. Fold line AC to GH, and then fold BD to GH.
3. Fold A and B down to lie on horizontal line EF.
4. Place thumbs inside two corner pockets and pull points A and B outward and down to make triangular points. (Be sure to check with illustration No. 4.)
5. From top point O of centerfold make diagonal folds to points A and B.
6. Fold bottom corners back.
7. Fold model in half (reversing centerfold).
8. Fold tail inward (a "squash fold"). Push thumb into point to keep the fold even and pinch the sides together.

Rabbit is taken from Papercrafts *by Ian Adair (David and Charles Holdings, Ltd., 1975).*

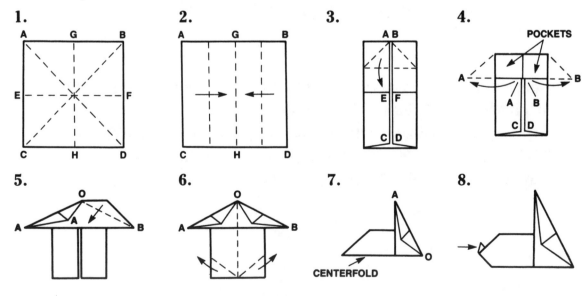

Write a Rebus

Help students visualize words and ideas by asking them to create a rebus: words and phrases made from pictures and plus (+) and minus (−) signs. Begin by showing students this rebus:

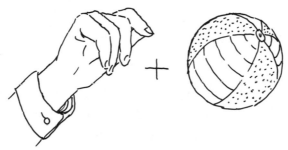

Ask them what word these two pictures might represent. Point out that *hand* and *ball* create the word *handball*. What pictures could students use to create *baseball*? *Football*? Discuss how one could draw a *base* and a *ball* to make *baseball*, a *foot* and a *ball* to make *football*. Point out how you can use plus and minus signs to add and subtract letters and syllables. To create the phrase *Be nice*, for example, students could draw this rebus:

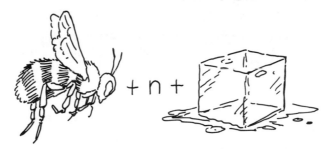

This rebus shows a *bee*, standing for the word *be*. To make the word *nice*, add *n* to *ice*.

Now have students create phrases or sentences in rebus form. When everyone is finished working, have students put their rebuses on the chalkboard for everyone to read.

Set the Scene

Another way to approach visualizing is to have students create dioramas or other three-dimensional representations of specific scenes from literature. Have students bring in shoe boxes. Begin the activity by reviewing with students the stories, poems, novels, and plays they have read during the year. Discuss scenes that were especially dramatic. List some of these scenes on the chalkboard.

Then direct students to select any one of the scenes from the chalkboard or any other scene that intrigues them. Have them sketch out the scene on a piece of paper and then transform their rough sketch into three-dimensional form. Students can use construction paper and small objects such as pebbles, sticks, and blocks in their scenes. Encourage students to experiment with depth and space by placing figures and objects in the background, middle ground, and foreground of their scenes. Students can use strips of fanned paper to anchor the figures and objects. When everyone is finished working, display the scenes for the class to share and discuss.

Glue here to position on wall.

Glue folded strip to cut-out figure along here.

Glue here to position on floor.

Back of cut-out princess

Name _____

Real Estate

Look carefully at the sixteen houses. Then answer these questions:

1. How many homes have only two windows and one door? _____

2. How many homes have no windows? _____

3. How many tents have doors, but no windows? _____

4. How many homes are *not* made with wood? _____

5. How many homes float? _____

6. How many homes have flags flying? _____

7. How many homes have 12 or more windows? _____

8. How many homes have a porch? _____

Alien Invasion

The Tombats have landed! Fortunately, they are friendly aliens. The Frombats have also landed—they're not so friendly. We'd like to send the Frombats back to their planet, Fromburgh, but we have trouble telling the Frombats from the Tombats. Can you help? Circle the Tombats in the bottom row.

All these are Tombats.

All these are Frombats.

Which of these are Tombats?

Twin Cat Bash

It's a special party just for twin cats. All of the cats that were invited have an identical twin who they brought along too. But three mischievous single cats snuck in! First, find the twelve pairs of identical twins. Then circle the three cats that have no twin. (Oh yes, and would you mind asking the single cats to scram?)

Welcome, Neighbor

Imagine that someone is moving to your city or town and doesn't know very much about your area. What would you tell them about your neighborhood? Create a brochure to make people moving to your area feel welcome. To help you gather your ideas, first answer the questions listed below.

1. Where is your city or town located? _____

_____

_____

2. List the schools in your area. _____

_____

_____

3. Tell about the activities for children. (Include parks, sports, clubs, etc.)

_____

_____

_____

4. What historic places are interesting to visit? _____

_____

_____

5. What are the best places to shop? _____

_____

_____

6. What are the best things about your town? _____

_____

_____

Stargazing

It's time to study the skies, but you won't need a telescope! Why? Because some stellar things are hidden in this puzzle. Find each of the heavenly bodies listed below. The words go across, down, and backwards. The first one is done for you.

Find these words:

~~Saturn~~	Orion	Earth	North Star	Moon
Sun	Milky Way	Mars	Venus	Pluto

```
M   N   O   R   T   H   S   T   A   R
  I   C   R   S   W   R   U   M   N   J
  L   H   I   S   Y   U   U   S   E   A
  K   A   O   T   U   L   P   A   A   Z
  Y   R   N   O   O   M   O   T   R   U
  W   L   Q   U   A   A   Y   U   T   Z
  A   E   L   O   B   R   O   R   H   O
  Y   S   P   W   B   S   U   N   E   V
```

3-D Doings

What a dull world we would have if everything was two-dimensional! We would all be flat—like paper! Study the five three-dimensional shapes below. For each one, think of five things that are the *same* shape and write them down. We have done the first ones for you.

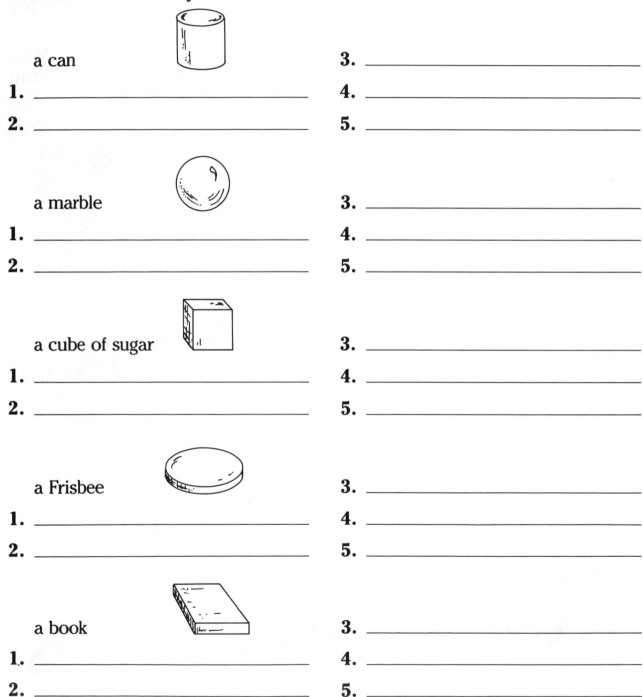

a can

1. _____
2. _____
3. _____
4. _____
5. _____

a marble

1. _____
2. _____
3. _____
4. _____
5. _____

a cube of sugar

1. _____
2. _____
3. _____
4. _____
5. _____

a Frisbee

1. _____
2. _____
3. _____
4. _____
5. _____

a book

1. _____
2. _____
3. _____
4. _____
5. _____

Name _____

Wrong Rhymes

Each word group contains three words that rhyme and one that does not rhyme. In the space provided, write the word that does not rhyme.

_____   **1.** can, fan, swam, man

_____   **2.** got, block, sock, frock

_____   **3.** stick, kicked, brick, lick

_____   **4.** fail, sign, hail, rail

_____   **5.** gall, side, hall, stall

_____   **6.** walk, balk, talk, fork

_____   **7.** kelp, help, sing, yelp

_____   **8.** peek, blind, hind, find

_____   **9.** hate, crate, lake, gate

_____   **10.** creak, snake, fake, make

_____   **11.** dumb, plumb, gum, jump

_____   **12.** fun, plum, sum, hum

_____   **13.** lace, base, taste, race

_____   **14.** spill, peel, seal, feel

_____   **15.** hoot, beet, flute, scoot

_____   **16.** hair, fair, bear, dead

_____   **17.** sock, croon, soon, tune

_____   **18.** glow, ate, flow, snow

_____   **19.** type, hike, ripe, pipe

_____   **20.** drop, sell, bell, smell

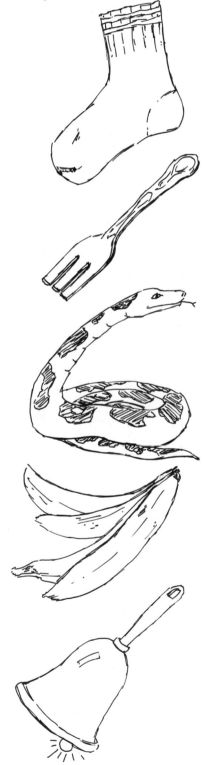

Look Again! 1

There are many different ways to look at one situation. For example, you can look at it through your own eyes, through the eyes of someone involved in the action, or through the eyes of someone outside the action. Rewrite the story below from the point of view indicated.

At school Laura was very tired and her mind was not on her work. In math class, the teacher called on her to give the answer to the first homework question, but even though she had done her work, she couldn't find her paper. The teacher was angry and the rest of the class laughed at her, which made her furious. She sunk lower and lower in her seat, trying to sink onto the floor. She couldn't remember a day as bad as this one.

Pretend you are Laura. Rewrite the story in the first person, using the pronoun *I*.

_____

_____

_____

_____

_____

_____

_____

_____

_____

_____

_____

_____

_____

_____

Name _____

Look Again! 2

I was walking home from the playground with my brother Ted, when it started to pour. Ted joked that it was "raining cats and dogs." Then we heard it: a faint mewing. As we approached a pine tree, the sound grew louder: mew . . . Mew . . . MEW!!! We looked up into the branches of the wet, giant tree and there we saw a tiny gray kitten with eyes as big as saucers . . .

Rewrite and complete the story from the kitten's point of view, using the pronoun *I*.

_____

_____

_____

_____

_____

_____

_____

_____

_____

_____

_____

_____

_____

_____

_____

_____

_____

Triangle Challenge

How many triangles can you find in this shape? Circle each triangle and write your total in the space below.

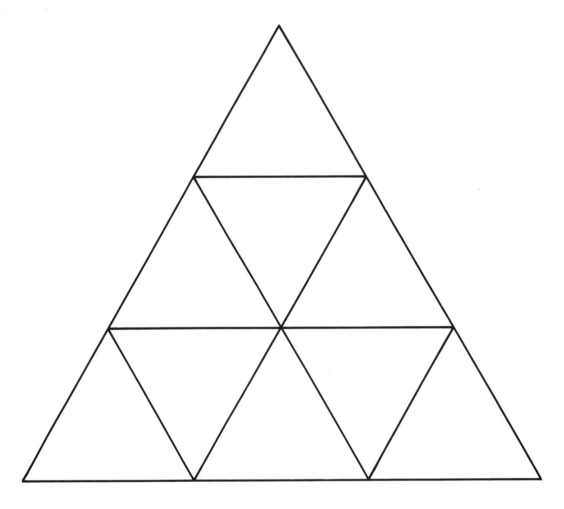

The number is:

_____

Classifying

When students classify, they examine a collection of facts and mentally place those facts in related groups. In other words, they process the facts or data, then organize them in some systematic way or according to some rule. Why is classifying an important skill? Because it brings order to students' thinking and helps them break a problem down into smaller, more manageable chunks.

The following activities are designed to boost classification skills. Because following directions is an important part of these activities, you might want to present them in the beginning of the day to remind students that following directions is important in *all* the work they do.

Turn-Around Numbers

This number activity challenges students to listen carefully to and follow your directions. It involves having students count backward, count forward, and skip lines. Ask students to take out a piece of lined paper. Then give them a series of directions. (You can select any sequence of steps you wish, but should keep in mind your students' abilities.) Here's an example:

1. Write the number 86. (86)

2. Count backward five numbers, and write the new number. (81)

3. Skip a line, count forward three numbers, skip another line, and write the new number. (84)

4. Count backward eight, forward two, skip two lines, and write the new number. (78)

5. Count forward nine, skip a line, and write the new number. (87)

6. Count backward eight, skip a line, count backward six, skip a line, and write the new number. (73)

7. Count forward three, skip a line, count forward ten, skip a line, and write the new number. (86)

8. Underline the new number. What is it? (86)

Continue the activity with different numbers and functions.

Quick Draw

You can use art as well as numbers to sharpen students' abilities to follow directions. Have each student take out a sheet of paper and a pencil. Explain to students that you are going to read a series of directions for them to follow. Then read these directions:

1. In the bottom left-hand corner of the paper, draw a square.

2. In the bottom right-hand corner of the paper, draw a square.

3. Draw a circle in the middle of each square.

4. Put a dot in the center of each circle.

5. Draw a line connecting the two squares.

6. Draw four triangles an inch from the top of the page.

7. Put an X in the first triangle on the right.

8. Draw a circle inside the second triangle from the right.

9. Draw a square inside the circle.

10. Put a square in the third triangle from the right.

11. Color in the last triangle.

12. Draw a circle around that triangle.

13. Draw a line across the middle of the page.

14. Use that line as one side of a rectangle.

15. Write your full name in script in the rectangle.

16. Draw a square directly above the rectangle.

17. Divide the square in half.

18. Color in half of the square.

Scrambled Sentences

Write this sentence on the board and have students copy it into their notebooks:

O xwen o my zoct xand O saiz, "Zoct, O broked my arml in hr plaxces." Hex saiz, "Wellp, tayl xout of th laces."

Then tell students to follow your directions to unscramble the sentence.

1. Change all the *Z's* to *D's*.

2. Cross off all the *X's*.

3. Add a *T* to the end of the second word, the beginning of the third word, and the beginning of the fifteenth word.

4. Change the three capital *O's* to capital *I's*.

5. Add a *P* to the beginning of the last word.

6. Cross off the last letter in the eleventh, thirteenth, and nineteenth words.

7. Put an *s* on the front of the twentieth word and cross off the last letter.

8. Add an *or* at the end of the fifth and ninth word.

9. Add an *ee* at the end of the fifteenth word.

10. Add *ose* at the end of the next to last word.

Corrected, the sentence reads:

I went to my doctor and I said, "Doctor, I broke my arm in three places." He said, "Well, stay out of those places."

QuizWhiz

This critical thinking activity helps students to recall and classify. Students will need a pencil and paper. You will need a watch, clock, or timer to let you know when five minutes have elapsed. Have students make a grid six spaces by six spaces on their paper. Down the left side, direct them to write one of these words in each space: *cities, authors, animals, celebrities,* and *food.* Across the top, have them write one of these letters in each space: T H I N K. Explain to students that they will have five minutes to fill in each category with a name or word that begins with each of the letters. If the letter is H, for example, under *cities* they might write *Houston;* under *authors, Hamilton, Virginia;* under *animals, hamster;* under *celebrities, Hanks, Tom;* under *food, hot dogs.* After the five minutes have elapsed, have students share their responses with the class. Give students a point for each answer given. The student with the most points wins! Continue the activity by changing the categories and letters. Encourage students to help you come up with them.

	T	H	I	N	K
cities		Houston			Kansas City
authors	Taylor, Mildred	Hamilton, Virginia			
animals	tiger	hamster		newt	kangaroo
celebrities	Turner, Tina	Hanks, Tom			
food	tuna	hot dogs		noodles	

Uncle Charley

This activity helps students build important classification skills. Begin by thinking of a category such as double letters. But don't tell the class what it is. Instead provide clues by talking about Uncle Charley. For example:

"Uncle Charley likes zucchini but he doesn't like oranges."

"He adores ferry rides, but hates taxis."

"He likes zippers and buttons, but is bothered by snaps."

"He would like to visit Russia and Greenland, but never California, New York, or Ohio."

"Does Uncle Charley like roses?"

"Tell me some more things he likes and dislikes."

The things Uncle Charley likes—zucchini, ferry rides, zippers, buttons, Russia, Greenland—all contain double letters. Continue the activity by having volunteers take turns thinking of new categories and presenting clues. Possible categories include specific letters, colors, temperatures, shapes, sizes, and geographic locations.

Alphabet Soup

Here's another fun and effective way to reinforce classification skills. Divide the class into two teams. Have each team form a line. Select one of the categories below and challenge Team A to create an alphabetized list of items in that category. For example, if the category is *snack foods* the first player on Team A might say "apples," the second might say "bananas," the third might say "corn chips," and so on. When a player on Team A is stumped, shift to Team B and challenge the first player to think of a word. If he or she is successful, continue down the line until a player on Team B is stumped. Award teams one point for each word they come up with. Keep score on the chalkboard. Play as many rounds with new categories as you like. The team with the most points wins the game!

Classification Categories

countries
places to avoid
things in a basement
creatures to avoid
   (real and imaginary)
snack foods
ways to bother people
things that grow
things you can put in your
   pocket
names of boys and girls
things you can put on a
   sandwich

careers or jobs
pop stars
items of clothing
movie stars
colors and hues
things bigger than a
   shoebox
vehicles
authors
things to do on a rainy day
sports stars

Type Cast

How would you categorize each of the following items? The first one is done for you. There is no "right" answer, so be prepared to explain your responses.

1. A violin is a type of   <u>instrument</u>

2. Cereal is a type of _____

3. Pine is a type of _____

4. A poodle is a type of _____

5. A pheasant is a type of _____

6. A cow is a type of _____

7. A hammer is a type of _____

8. A hyacinth is a type of _____

9. A butterfly is a type of _____

10. Platinum is a type of _____

11. Jogging is a type of _____

12. Brown is a type of _____

13. A sonnet is a type of _____

14. Flying is a type of _____

15. A heifer is a type of _____

16. Zucchini is a type of _____

17. An arm is a type of _____

18. A football player is a type of _____

19. A mystery is a type of _____

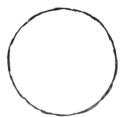

20. A circle is a type of _____

Are We There Yet?

In the space below, write directions from your classroom to any place in the school building such as the cafeteria, the library, or the gym. Do not write the name of your destination. Instead, write the line: "And then you are there." When you have finished writing your mystery directions, exchange papers with a classmate and create a map from his or her directions. In the space provided, write the name of the destination. Exchange papers with that same classmate to see if you and your partner were correct.

Directions: _____

_____

_____

_____

_____

_____

_____

Map:

The destination is: _____

Name _____

Save Yourself!

Below is a map of the Kingdom of Og, a sad and dangerous land. Unfortunately, you were stranded in Og when your camels went into revolt. Now the fierce residents of Og are after you, seeking your precious cargo of peanut butter—the rarest and most sought-after item in Og. You must escape to the land of Zog. The residents of Zog hate peanut butter and, therefore, won't bother you. Fortunately, you have a map to lead you there. Draw your path in pencil; mark each stop with an X. Follow these directions.

Directions:

Go northeast four miles to the mountains. Head four miles due north to the castle, where you'll make a quick stop for lunch. Then travel eight miles northwest to the lake, where you'll take a refreshing dip. Then go sixteen miles east to the oasis for a rest. Do not go south or you will end up in the quicksand. From the oasis, continue east five miles to the bike stand, where you'll hop on a bike and pedal three miles north to Zog. Good luck!

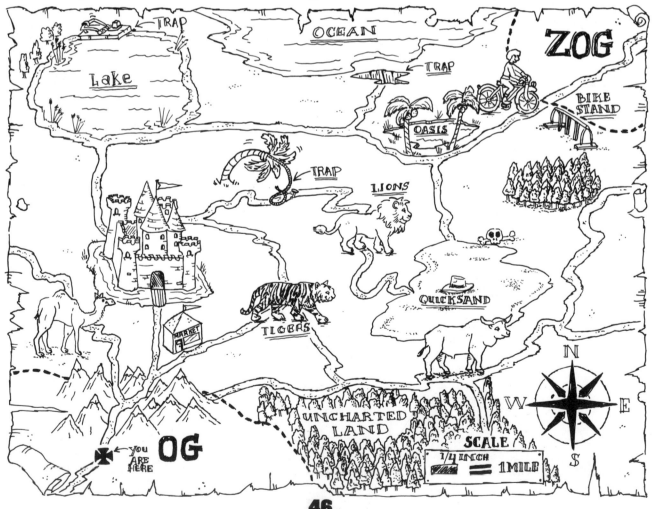

Travel Log

Below is a list of well-known places. Divide the places into groups. Classify them anyway you like. Note: The groups may vary in size; you need not use all of the places.

Amazon River	France	Israel
Japan	China	Alaska
India	Death Valley	Cape Canaveral
Barbados	Spain	Egypt
Niagara Falls	Kansas	Australia
Kenya	Iran	the Everglades
the Grand Canyon	London	Vietnam
the Mississippi River	New York City	Florida
Hawaii	Mexico	Paris

Here's an example:

Super Vacation Places

Hawaii	France	Australia
Mexico	Barbados	Florida

Group 1 classification: _____

Places: _____

_____

Group 2 classification: _____

Places: _____

_____

Group 3 classification: _____

Places: _____

_____

Name _____

Clean-Up Time!

Each of these lists has one item that does not belong.
Clean up the list by crossing out that item. In the
space provided explain why you think that item is out
of place. The first one is done for you.

1. zebra, lion, elephant, ~~kitten~~ The kitten is not a wild animal.

2. tack, pliers, wrench, screwdriver _____

3. soccer, tennis, track, bowling _____

4. plum, melon, peach, apricot _____

5. New Mexico, Albany, Utah, Vermont _____

6. silver, rubies, brass, iron _____

7. pen, pencil, crayon, ruler _____

8. drums, oboe, saxophone, flute _____

9. leave, arrive, depart, go _____

10. horse, puppy, chick, duckling _____

11. newspaper, radio, book, magazine _____

12. eyes, nose, mouth, foot _____

Sequencing and Predicting

Learning to organize facts and data in a systematic, sequential way is a complex skill. But this skill is vital to logical thought. Through sequencing, students are able to connect facts and events in a meaningful way. Once they see those connections, they are better able to use their prior knowledge to predict what might happen next in a story or a series of events, or how well a particular strategy might work in solving a problem.

The activities in this section will sharpen students' skills in sequencing and predicting.

Game Makin'

Here's a super way to hone students' critical thinking skills: Have children design their own theme-based board games. Challenge students to make every element of their game—the purpose, the board, the playing pieces, etc.—relate to the theme that they choose. For example, if the theme is Outer Space, the purpose of the game could be to travel via "spacecraft" from planet to planet. Players might move from Pluto to Neptune by correctly answering a question about the solar system. The first player to make it safely back to earth is the winner.

Assign each student a partner. Give children a big block of time to brainstorm their games' themes, purposes, rules, and how the games will be made. Students may also wish to use this time to further research their themes.

Next, have students create the games. Provide an array of material including thick pieces of cardboard (for the boards), glue, scissors, markers, crayons, index cards, dice, buttons, etc.

When students are done, have them trade games with their classmates. Later, discuss the games. Which ones were particularly exciting to play and why? Store all of the games for children to play during their free time.

Fortune Cookies

Sharpen your students' predicting skills by having them make paper "fortune cookies." Begin by asking students to think about the books they read throughout the year. Write the titles of several of them on the chalkboard.

Give each student a piece of tan paper about 6-inches by 6-inches. Then direct them to select a character from one of the books and, based on what happened in the story, write a prediction for that character. Have students write their predictions on small strips of white paper, which are placed inside the tan paper. They then fold and tape closed their "fortune cookies."

Collect the cookies and place them in a container. Invite students to take turns picking the cookies, identifying the works of literature and characters, and discussing the validity of the predictions.

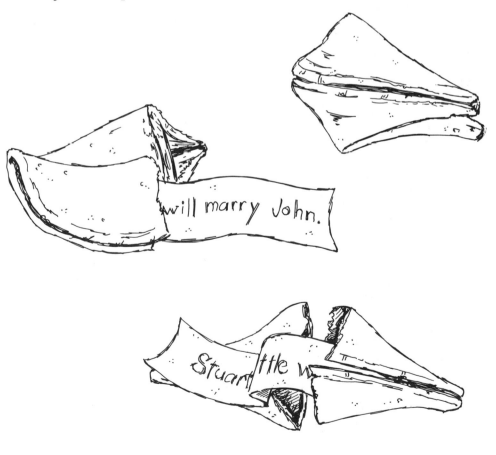

So What's New?

Here's another way to reinforce the critical thinking skill of predicting. Begin by asking each student to bring in two newspaper articles. Collect the articles and read the headlines to the class. Then invite students to predict the contents of the articles based on the headlines. Read the first paragraphs of the articles to see if they were correct.

The activity can be extended by challenging students to write the article, based only on the headline.

Name _____

Happily Ever After?

Ever wish a favorite book had an extra chapter that told you what happened to the main characters? Well this is your chance to write it! Choose a book you especially like. Then decide what you want to happen in your extra chapter. To help you gather ideas, create a word cluster around the last key event in the story. First write that key event in the center circle and the names of the main characters in the middle circles. Then brainstorm ways that event might affect the lives of those characters. Write things that might happen to them in the outside circles. After you have organized your thoughts, write the extra chapter on the back of this paper. Does everyone live happily ever after?

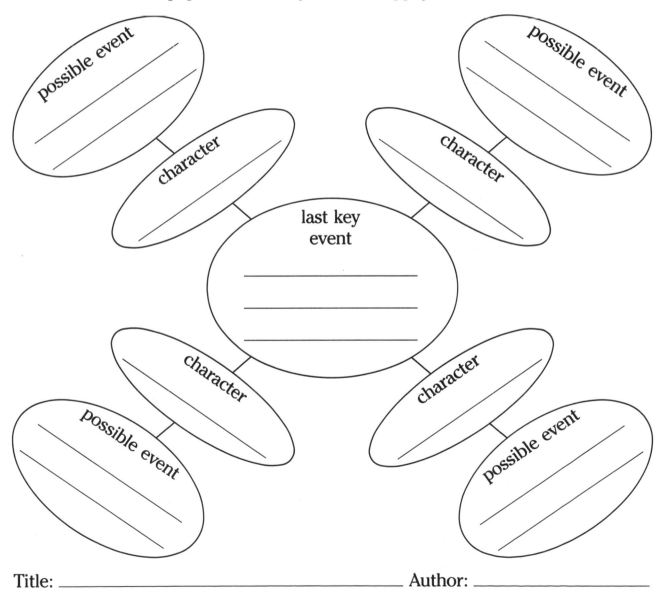

Title: _____ Author: _____

The Survival Game

Oh no! Your watch stopped and you missed the tour boat back to civilization. Looks like you'll be spending a while on an uninhabited tropical island. Below are 30 items that might come in handy during your stay. Rank them in order of most important (1) to least important (30). Be prepared to discuss your answers.

_____ a bag of dried fruit

_____ 6 gallons of drinking water

_____ a jackknife

_____ a Walkman and tapes

_____ 10 bunches of bananas

_____ 10 cans of vegetables

_____ matches

_____ a copy of *Treasure Island*

_____ a blanket

_____ a bathing suit

_____ a deck of playing cards

_____ a hunting knife

_____ a can opener

_____ chewing gum

_____ a walkie-talkie

_____ soap

_____ ketchup and mustard

_____ a change of clothes

_____ a Frisbee

_____ a sack of potatoes

_____ a book called *Eatable Tropical Plants*

_____ a flashlight

_____ a camera

_____ rope

_____ a compass

_____ 10 pounds of hamburger

_____ a device that converts salt water to drinking water

_____ a raincoat

_____ a comb

_____ a radio

Attention!

Below are lists of four items. Each list can be ordered in many different ways. Arrange each list in a way that makes sense to you. Write your explanation on the line provided.

For example: birdhouse, house, pup tent, castle

You might arrange the items in order of size—from smallest to biggest: birdhouse, pup tent, house, castle. Or, you might choose to arrange them in alphabetical order: birdhouse, castle, house, pup tent. The choice is yours!

1. hour, second, day, minute _____

_____

2. Elizabeth Atkinson, Carlos Diaz, Andrea Martin, Bob Kin _____

_____

3. dawn, dusk, midnight, high noon _____

_____

4. seed, bud, flower, fruit _____

_____

5. neck, head, feet, knees _____

_____

6. California, Pennsylvania, Alaska, Hawaii _____

_____

7. peach, pea, cabbage, watermelon _____

_____

8. adult, toddler, baby, teenager _____

_____

Palindrome Challenge

A palindrome is a word, phrase, or sentence that reads the same backwards as it does forwards. Probably the most famous examples are *Madam, I'm Adam* and Napoleon's *Able was I ere I saw Elba. Rise to vote, sir* and *A war at Tarawa* are also palindromes.

Able was I ere I saw Elba.

Create your own original palindrome of at least three words. Be sure it makes sense!

My palindrome:

_____

Use this space as scratch paper.

Name _____

The Deal of a Lifetime

You're in charge of an advertising campaign! First
decide what product you want to sell. It can be a
popular item or one that exists only in your
imagination. Plan a sixty-second television
commercial. Sketch each scene of your commercial in
the squares below. Under each scene, write the words
your characters and/or announcer will say.

Name _____

Puzzle Pattern

The following designs have been created by moving a piece of the puzzle. Solve the puzzle by predicting how it must change to continue the pattern.

Study squares 1 and 2. How did 1 change to create 2?

1.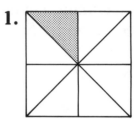

2.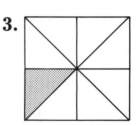

Look at square 3. How is it different from 2? Predict how 4 will change.

3.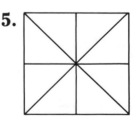

Look at 4 to see if you were correct. Based on this pattern, what will 5 look like? Fill in 5.

4.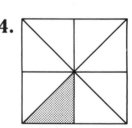

5.

Super Challenge Create your own changing pattern on the back of this paper. Then trade papers with a friend to see if he or she is able to predict how *your* pattern changed.

Name _____

Big Questions

Answer the following questions. There is no "right" answer. When you finish, compare your responses with a classmate to see how your opinions are the same and different.

1. How would life be different if the sun never set? _____

_____

_____

2. How would life be different if people could only get from place to place by walking? _____

_____

_____

3. How would life be different if you were a bug instead of a human? _____

_____

_____

4. How would life be different if there was no gravity? _____

_____

_____

5. How would life be different if the sky was green? _____

_____

_____

6. How would life be different if the United States, Europe, Africa, China, etc. were all connected and there was only one land mass? _____

_____

_____

More Big Questions

Answer the following questions. There is no "right" answer. When you finish, compare your responses with a classmate to see how your opinions are the same and different.

1. How would life be different if there was no more snow anywhere in the world? _____

_____

2. How would life be different if the past could be relived? _____

_____

_____

3. How would life be different if no one needed to sleep? _____

_____

_____

4. How would life be different if we all looked and dressed the same? _____

_____

_____

5. How would life be different if there was no government in the United States?

_____

_____

6. How would life be different if dinosaurs were still alive? _____

_____

_____

7. How would life be different if animals could talk? _____

_____

_____

Inferring and Drawing Conclusions

The activities that follow will help students practice their skills in inferring and drawing conclusions. When we infer, we use prior knowledge and evidence to come to a conclusion about an object or an event. Critical thinkers are adept at distinguishing between conclusions based on assumptions and those based on observable fact.

As you work through the nine activities in this section, encourage students to formulate procedures for completing them. At the end of each activity, have students explain exactly how they arrived at their solutions. What information helped them draw conclusions? How did they make inferences?

Fictionary

This entertaining activity helps students become more adept at making inferences and drawing conclusions. You will need a good dictionary, a fish bowl or similar container, paper, and pencils or pens. Explain to students that they are going to try to fool their classmates by creating phony dictionary definitions.

First select a word from the dictionary that students do not know, such as *propolis*. Then challenge students to make up definitions based on the word's root, suffix, prefix, the way it sounds, or what it reminds them of. For *propolis*, for example, a student might suggest "city of lost propellers," since *prop* sounds like *propeller* and *polis* sounds like the ending of many Greek words such as *Acropolis*. Have students write their fake definitions on slips of paper along with their names. Meanwhile, you write the *real* definition. (*Propolis*, for example, means "a brownish, waxy material collected by bees from the buds of trees and used as cement.")

Collect the definitions and mix them in a fish bowl. Read all of the definitions to the class. Have each student vote for the definition he or she thinks is the real one. Give students one point for each vote their phony definitions receive. Play as many rounds as you like. The student with the most points wins.

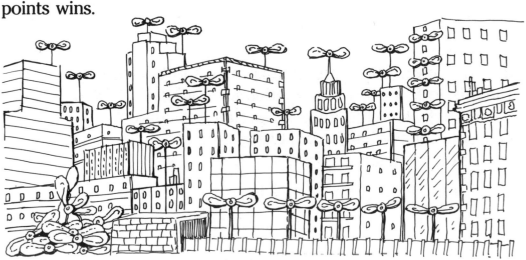

Familiar Face, New Place

Here's an activity that helps students draw conclusions about what they have read and studied. Review the fictional characters and historical figures that students have encountered in books throughout the year. Create a list on the chalkboard. The list might go something like this: Paul Bunyan, Johnny Appleseed, Laura Ingalls Wilder, Christopher Columbus, Ramona Quimby. Discuss which people are real and which are imaginary. Ask students to choose one of the people and make a list of their characteristics. For example, if the student chose Laura Ingalls Wilder, he or she might write: strong, brave, honest, pioneer, family oriented, smart, mischievous, etc.

After students have completed their lists, challenge each child to think of a situation the character might find him- or herself in and write a short story about it. Students can move their characters backward or forward in time, or place them in a new locale. However, they should be careful to retain the qualities of their character. Encourage students to ask themselves: "Is this really something so-and-so would do?" After everyone is done writing, have children read their stories aloud. Or, you might want to publish a class anthology to send home to parents.

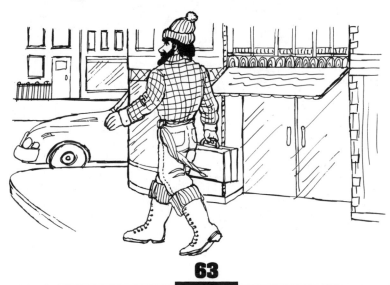

Who Dun It?

Select a story that has a suspenseful ending. Begin reading the story aloud to the class. Stop the story at a crucial point. Tell students that their task is to solve the mystery of the story's ending. Arrange students in groups of five or six, depending on the number of characters in the story. Have one student in each group act as a detective and others as each of the main characters from the work. Make sure that everyone has a role. Challenge the groups to decide how the story will end. Then have each group act out its ending for the class. Ask students to explain how they reached their conclusions; encourage them to support their claims by citing details from the story.

After all the skits are completed, read the rest of the story to the class. Compare the author's ending to the students' endings.

What Happens Next?

Here's another effective way to encourage students to draw conclusions. Read a story aloud and stop at a crucial point. Then have students complete the story, drawing conclusions based on what you have read so far. Make this activity extra challenging by selecting a story with an ending that is open to some interpretation.

After students have completed their writing, invite them to share their endings with the class. After all the students have read their endings, decide, by a show of hands, which ending seems the most logical. Have students point out specific references in the story that led them to conclude that the plot might be resolved in this way.

Then read the rest of the story and compare the students' endings with the author's ending. How are they the same? How are they different? Did anyone predict the real ending?

That's Funny!

Have students bring in favorite comic strips from the newspaper. Make sure that they clip comics that have at least four panels. Cut off the last panel and redistribute the comics to other students. (Make sure that no student receives the comic he or she brought in.) Then challenge students to complete the strip by drawing the last panel and filling in appropriate dialogue. Display the results and ask students to justify their conclusions.

Variation: White-out the dialogue of several single-panel comics. Photocopy them and distribute one to each child. Challenge students to fill in appropriate dialogue. Share these with the class. Discuss the visual clues that students relied on to create their dialogue.

Constant Confusion

Mr. and Mrs. Dinkledorff have a problem. They have identical quintuplets—
Jessica, Jennifer, Justina, Judith, and Jackie—and they can't tell the babies apart.
Read the clues below. Then give the overworked Dinkledorffs a hand by writing
each baby's name in the space provided.

CLUES

A. Judith is sitting between Jessica and Justina.
B. Jessica has no one on *her* right-hand side.
C. Jackie, the firstborn, always sits in front.

3. _____

4. _____

5. _____

1. _____

2. _____

Name _____

Make a Wish

Every week, Jeffrey cleans out the wishing well at the park. Use these clues to figure out how many pennies, nickels, and dimes he finds this week. Write your answer on the correct basket.

CLUES

1. He finds at least one penny, one nickel, and one dime.
2. He has a total of 14 coins.
3. The coins add up to 56¢.
4. He has more nickels than dimes.
5. He has the same number of pennies as nickels.

PENNIES
How many? _____

NICKEL
How many? _____

DIMES
How many? _____

Loopy Language

An *idiom* is an expression that has an accepted meaning very different from its literal meaning. For example, the words *hit the road* literally mean "slap the ground," but most of us take the phrase to mean "time to go." Likewise, if you tell a person that you *bought a lemon,* you're probably not talking about a piece of fruit. Rather, the idiom means you got stuck with something, such as a car or appliance, that doesn't work properly. Below are fifteen idioms. On the left, write the literal meaning for each. On the right, write the accepted meaning of each.

Idiom	Literal Meaning	Accepted Meaning
1. take the cake		
2. on the blink		
3. catch some z's		
4. bury the hatchet		
5. a real turkey		
6. pulling your leg		
7. turn the tables		
8. caught red-handed		
9. crazy as a bedbug		
10. chill out		
11. bite the bullet		
12. pig out		
13. rubberneck		
14. skin of your teeth		
15. chew the fat		

Redesigning the States

America is divided into fifty wonderful states, but what if it wasn't? What if it were up to you to "design" the United States? Below is a map of America. Use a pencil to divide it up into as many states as you like. The states can be any size and shape. Give each state a fantastic new name. When you're done, color in your map. On the back of this paper write a paragraph or two explaining why you chose the design and names that you did. Then share your vision of America with a friend!

The United States

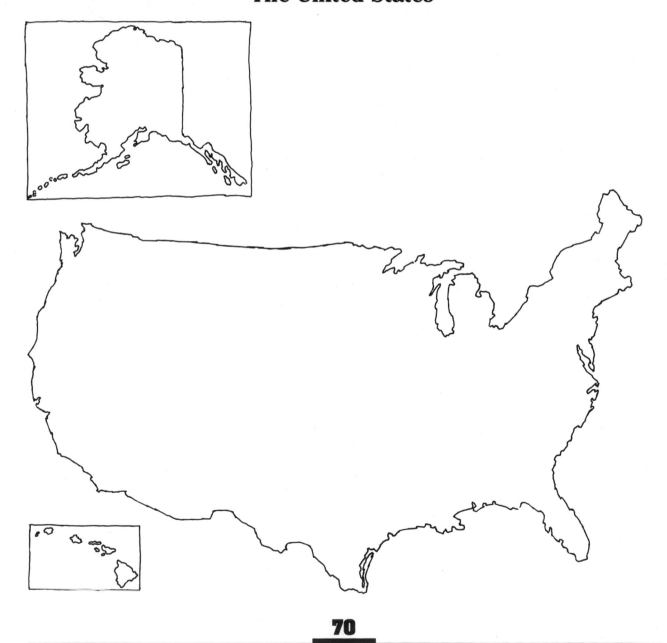

Evaluating

The activities in this section will help students learn to form opinions that are backed up by sound reasoning.

Before students begin working, remind them that evaluating a person, problem-solving strategy, or situation consists of making a judgment—one based not on personal preference, but on observable facts. For example, if a student gives a book an unfavorable evaluation, he or she should be able to say more than, "I just didn't like it." An evaluation arrived at through critical thinking would sound more like this: "I didn't like it because the ending was confusing."

In "Sports Hall of Fame" (page 72), "My Hero" (page 76), and "Stamp of Fame" (page 78), students evaluate a person's qualities. In "Fact or Opinion" (Page 75), they evaluate ideas or things; and in "Undercover Work" (page 79) and "My Book Review" (page 81), they evaluate books.

Name _____

The Sports Hall of Fame

Imagine that you have been asked to nominate a person for possible induction into the Sports Hall of Fame. Who would you nominate and why? Your choice can be a professional athlete from the past or present, a friend, a parent, a coach, or teacher. Complete the form below.

A. Name of person nominated: _____

B. Main sport that he or she plays: _____

_____

C. Number of years playing the sport: _____

D. Three reasons why the person should be inducted into the Sports Hall of Fame:

    1. _____

    _____

    _____

    2. _____

    _____

    _____

    3. _____

    _____

    _____

What Does It Represent?

Throughout Asia, a crane represents good luck. That's because the crane is a *symbol,* a concrete object that stands for an idea: good luck. Similarly, an olive branch symbolizes peace and a white flag symbolizes surrender. Write a sentence to explain what each of the following symbols means to you.

a dove

an eagle

_____

_____

the American flag

a red rose

_____

_____

a fox

an owl

_____

_____

a wedding ring

a four-leaf clover

_____

_____

Create Your Own Symbol

If you could choose one object to represent *you,* what would it be? A sports fanatic might choose a pair of sneakers; an aspiring writer might choose a book; and a nature lover might choose a tree. Take some time to think of a personal symbol. Draw it in the box below. Then write why you selected it to represent yourself.

Personal Symbol: _____

Why I chose my symbol: _____

_____

_____

_____

_____

_____

Fact or Opinion?

A fact is something that cannot change. Facts are true. *Halloween occurs on October 31* is a fact. In contrast, an *opinion* is a personal belief that can change and does not have to be true. Many people may share the same opinion, but that does not make it a fact. *Halloween is the best holiday* is an opinion. In the blanks below, write *fact* if the statement is a fact and *opinion* if it is an opinion. Be ready to explain your answers.

_____ 1. *Island of the Blue Dolphins* is a great book.

_____ 2. By the time a child is five years old, he or she knows about 5,000 words.

_____ 3. Charles Schultz's best character is Charlie Brown.

_____ 4. Rainbows are created when drops of water are hit by light and form prisms.

_____ 5. Mercury, Venus, Earth, Mars, Jupiter, Saturn, Uranus, Neptune, and Pluto are planets.

_____ 6. Sixth grade is more fun than fifth grade.

_____ 7. The first home television set, built in 1928, had a screen that measured 3 inches by 4 inches.

_____ 8. George Washington's face appears on the 25-cent piece.

_____ 9. The Empire State Building can sway up to 2 inches in high winds.

_____ 10. Americans eat more than two billion pounds of pasta a year.

_____ 11. Cats make nice pets.

_____ 12. No two people have the same fingerprints.

_____ 13. Sign language is the language used third most often in America, after English and Spanish.

_____ 14. You should use mustard on hot dogs and ketchup on hamburgers.

_____ 15. Red and blue are primary colors.

_____ 16. Pretzels taste great when you eat them one at a time.

_____ 17. The New York Mets won the World Series in 1969.

_____ 18. My nose is too long.

_____ 19. Jupiter is the largest planet in our solar system.

_____ 20. Alligators and crocodiles are both endangered animals.

My Hero!

List the five people you admire most. These people can be from the past or the present.

Hero **1.** _____

Hero **2.** _____

Hero **3.** _____

Hero **4.** _____

Hero **5.** _____

Think of a trait that all the people you admire have in common. Write it below.

_____

_____

_____

Now, think of a special quality that makes each of the people unique? Write a different trait for each of them below.

Hero **1.** _____

Hero **2.** _____

Hero **3.** _____

Hero **4.** _____

Hero **5.** _____

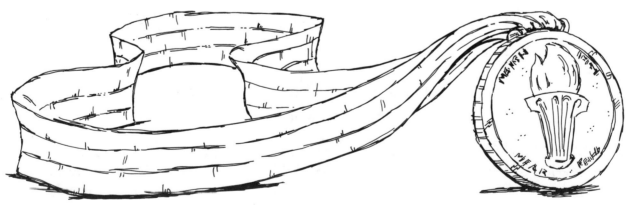

Our Family's Coat of Arms

A family coat of arms is a shield with pictures that represent your family. For example, if your family lives in the mountains, loves baseball, and travels a lot, your coat of arms might include a mountain, a baseball diamond, and a car with suitcases on its roof. Think about what makes your family unique. Then design a family coat of arms below. Be sure to include a family motto!

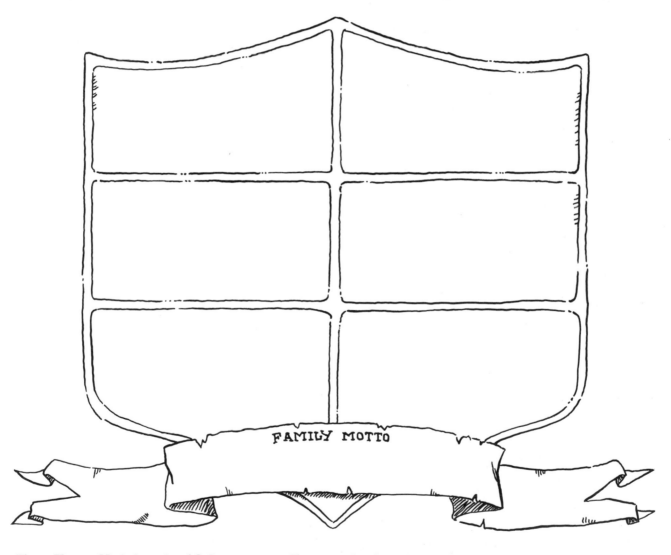

FAMILY MOTTO

Fun Fact: Knights in 12th-century Europe had individual patterns put on their battle shields and their coats. That is why a family crest is called a "coat of arms."

Stamp of Fame

Many famous people have been honored by being placed on stamps. The only rule is that the person can no longer be living. Decide what person from the past you would honor this way. Then create the stamp. Include a picture of the person, the person's birth date, some objects that represent the person, and the stamp's value. Draw your stamp below.

Name _____

Undercover Work

Select a book you haven't read before. Examine the cover, thumb through the pages, and look at the illustrations. Then see if you can answer the **who, what, where, when, why,** and **how** questions listed below. Finally, based on your undercover work, explain why you would or would not choose to read the book.

Who do I think this book is about? _____

_____

What do I think this book is about? _____

_____

Where do I think this book takes place? _____

_____

When do I think this story might take place? _____

_____

How do I feel about what I have discovered? _____

_____

Why do I feel this way? _____

_____

I would/would not read this book because _____

_____

_____

_____

_____

_____

_____

Name _____

Buy My Gizmo!

You've just invented a fabulous product! Now, you need to tell folks about it. Plan an advertising campaign for your product by filling in the information below.

Product name: _____

Product description: _____

_____

Describe the type of person that you think will buy your product: _____

_____

_____

Write a slogan for your product: _____

_____

Choose a famous person to endorse your product: _____

Tell why you chose him or her: _____

_____

Name a TV show you are planning to advertise during: _____

Tell why you chose it: _____

_____

Name a magazine you are planning to advertise in: _____

Tell why you chose it: _____

_____

Think of another way to interest people in your product and write it here: _____

_____

_____

Name _____

My Book Review

Write your own book review! First, pick a book and read it carefully. Then answer the questions below. When you're done, share your book review with the class.

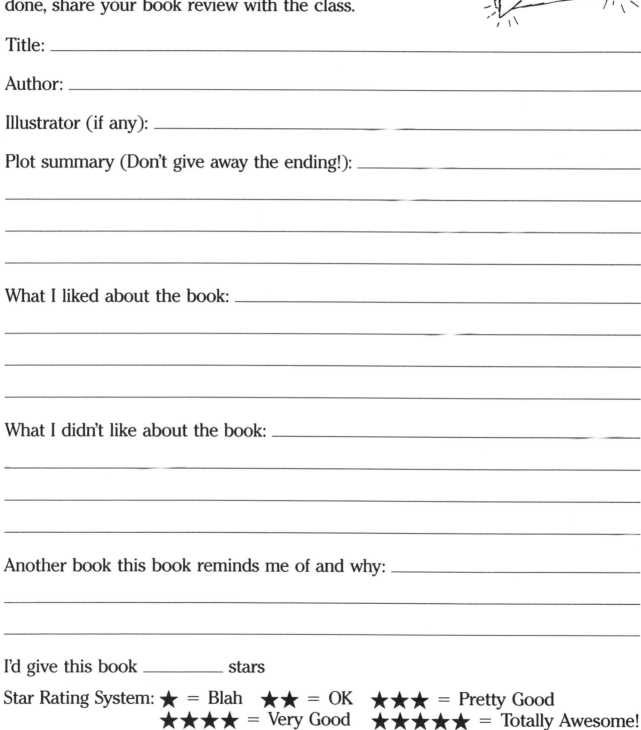

GOLD STAR REVIEW

Title: _____

Author: _____

Illustrator (if any): _____

Plot summary (Don't give away the ending!): _____

_____

_____

_____

What I liked about the book: _____

_____

_____

_____

What I didn't like about the book: _____

_____

_____

_____

Another book this book reminds me of and why: _____

_____

_____

I'd give this book _____ stars

Star Rating System: ★ = Blah ★★ = OK ★★★ = Pretty Good
★★★★ = Very Good ★★★★★ = Totally Awesome!

Name _____

Me! Me! Me!

You evaluate books, places, and things every day.
Now, take a look at yourself by answering each of the
following questions:

1. I am especially good at _____

2. I am a good friend because I _____
_____

3. People can trust me because I _____
_____

4. One of the best things about me is _____
_____

5. I am fun to be with when I _____
_____

6. I help my parents by _____

7. I help my friends by _____

8. I help my community by _____
_____

9. I try to make the world a better place by _____
_____

10. I like myself because I _____
_____

Analyzing

When we ask students to analyze, we ask them to break up a whole into its parts so as to study its nature and determine its essential features. By analyzing a piece of literature, for example, students may determine its main idea and all the important details related to that idea. By studying the parts of a story, concept, or problem, students are better able to understand the whole. These activities will help students become more adept at analyzing ideas and information.

After you've explained analysis to your students, try modeling the process by working through any one of the activities in this section. Think aloud as you work, to demonstrate your reasoning. Encourage students to think along with you and share their responses.

A Million-and-One Uses

Here's an activity that encourages students to take a fresh look at some familiar objects. Write the names of these objects on slips of paper and put them in a hat:

○ a piece of paper
○ a sheet
○ a pillow
○ a book
○ a chair
○ a cup
○ a piece of string
○ a box
○ a rubber band

Divide students into small groups. Have each group draw a slip from the hat. Then give that group 15 minutes to brainstorm new uses for that object. For example, if the group selected *a piece of paper,* its list might go something like this: fold into a fan to keep cool, fold into a cup for drinking, crumple into a ball to play catch, use as a bookmark, etc.

After the brainstorming session, invite the groups to share their lists with the class.

Transformations

Study the first pair of shapes in each example. Think about how A changes into B. Then take a look at C. Which of the six numbered shapes changes in relation to C in the same way that A changed to B? Find that shape. Circle the number of your answer.

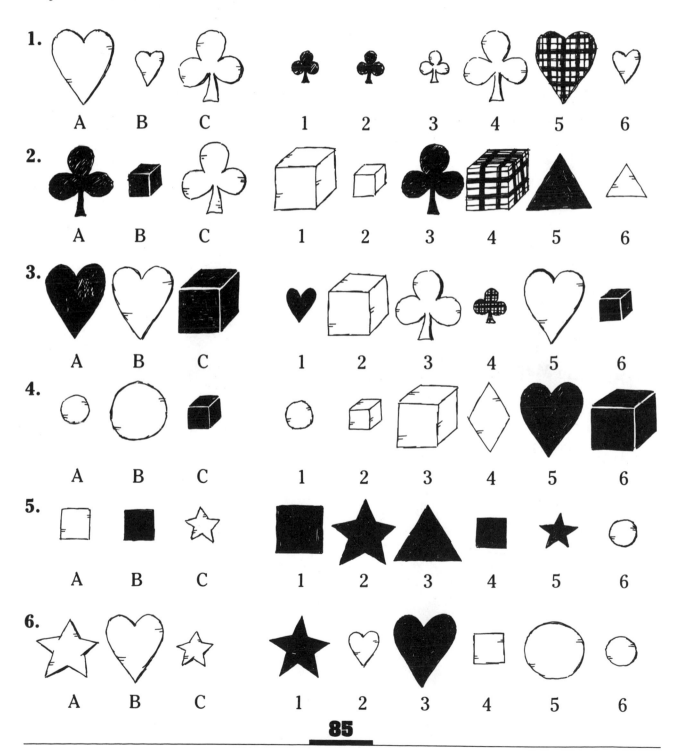

The Magic Number Is . . .

Marissa the Magician makes magic numbers appear. Read the clues to discover the magic number.

1. The number has two digits.

2. The number is less than fifty.

3. The number can be evenly divided by two.

4. The sum of the number's digits is 9.

5. If you subtract the first digit of the number from the second digit you get 3.

And the Magic Number is:

Name _____

Scavenger Hunt

Guess what! You're going on a scavenger hunt and you don't even have to leave your desk. Think of something that fits each of the descriptions below and write it in the blank. The first one has been done for you. When you're finished, trade papers with a classmate to see what he or she collected.

1. Something you toss: _ball_ _____

2. Something that is messy: _____

3. Something that changes shape: _____

4. Something that you should not walk on: _____

5. Something that you shake: _____

6. Something that smells fantastic: _____

7. Something that you heat: _____

8. Something that changes color: _____

9. Something that you freeze: _____

10. Something that you stir: _____

11. Something that is loud: _____

12. Something that grows: _____

13. Something that opens: _____

14. Something you carry: _____

15. Something that squeaks: _____

Amazing Analogies

Analogies look like this: **yolk : egg :: pit : cherry**

You read this analogy by saying: "Yolk is to egg as pit is to cherry." Analogies show relationships between pairs of words. In this example, the relationship is part is to whole: a yolk is *part* of an egg, and a pit is *part* of a cherry.

Complete the analogies below. Then write the analogy statement. The first one has been done for you.

1. dry : desert :: wet : Ocean / Dry is to desert as wet is to ocean.

2. palm : hand :: sole : _____

3. three : triangle :: four : _____

4. Venus : planet :: poodle : _____

5. pears : trees :: potatoes : _____

6. turkey : Thanksgiving :: witch : _____

7. shades : windows :: rugs : _____

8. swimming : water :: sledding : _____

9. grapes : cluster :: bananas : _____

10. teacher : chalk :: artist : _____

11. book : read :: television : _____

12. sugar : sweet :: lemon : _____

Odd Couples

The following pairs may seem mismatched at first
glance, but they actually have *a lot* in common. Think
about these "odd couples." Then write down all the
things they have in common with their "mates." When
you're done, compare your responses with a classmate's.

1. kitten/baby _____

_____

2. computer/typewriter _____

_____

3. magazine/radio _____

_____

4. worm/snail _____

_____

5. water/wind _____

_____

6. bubbles/balloons _____

_____

7. spring/birth _____

_____

8. 3/7 _____

_____

9. lion/elephant _____

_____

10. tomatoes/cherries _____

_____

Linking Lines

Bartholomew Bottlesworth writes wonderful tales. Unfortunately, he's experiencing a terrible case of writer's block. He managed to write only four sentences of his new story. Can you help? Think of a storyline that will somehow link these four sentences. Then finish writing Bartholomew's tale. Don't forget to give the story a great title.

Title _____

By Bartholomew Bottlesworth and _____

Once upon a time, there was a boy who lived at the top of a mountain. _____

_____

_____

_____

_____

But his grandmother's house was very far away. _____

_____

_____

_____

_____

It rained and rained. _____

_____

_____

_____

_____ And the boy lived happily ever after.

Name _____

Novel Conflict

Conflict is a struggle or fight between opposing forces. There are three kinds of conflict:

1. a person struggling against another person or group
2. a person struggling against nature
3. a person struggling against his or her own feelings

Almost all the books you read are about conflict. Choose a novel you have read recently. Explore its conflict(s) by answering the following questions.

Title _____ Author _____

Describe the main conflict. _____

_____

Which of the three kinds of conflict is it? _____

_____

How is the main conflict resolved? _____

_____

Are there any other conflicts in the novel? If so, list them below.

Conflict 2 _____

_____

Which kind of conflict is it? _____

How is the conflict resolved? _____

_____

Conflict 3 _____

_____

Which kind of conflict is it? _____

How is the conflict resolved? _____

_____

Rainy Days and Sundays

Not every day can be exciting—some boring rainy days and Sundays slip in there, too! In the space below, describe a situation you find boring. Then list some ways to make the situation better!

It is boring when _____

_____

I make this boring time exciting by:

1. _____

_____

2. _____

_____

3. _____

_____

4. _____

_____

5. _____

_____

6. _____

_____

Anagram Adventure

An anagram is a word that is made by rearranging the letters of another word. For example, here are four anagrams from the word *post*:

stop   **pots**   **tops**   **spot**

Form as many anagrams as you can from each of these words:

dare   teas   meat

_____   _____   _____

_____   _____   _____

_____   _____   _____

_____   _____   _____

_____   _____   _____

peach   stale   pans

_____   _____   _____

_____   _____   _____

_____   _____   _____

_____   _____   _____

trace   acre   slip

_____   _____   _____

_____   _____   _____

_____   _____   _____

_____   _____   _____

Scoop of the Century!

Your editor at *The Daily Planet* has given you the assignment of a lifetime: *Interview a famous person from history.* Choose a person you would like to interview and prepare five questions for him or her. Then ask a classmate to pretend to be that person. Write the interview in the spaces below. (Don't forget to use quotation marks to show dialogue.)

_____

_____

_____

_____

_____

_____

_____

_____

_____

_____

_____

_____

_____

_____

_____

_____

_____

_____

_____

Divide and Conquer

Below are a series of shapes. Analyze each shape to see how many different ways you can divide it into four equal pieces. The first square is done for you. (Note: You may not be able to divide a shape into four equal pieces at all.)

1.

2.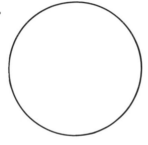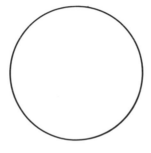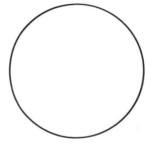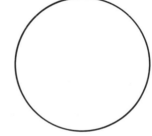

3.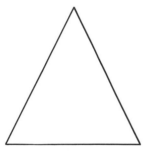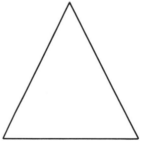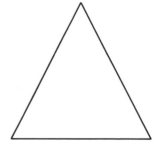

4.

A Great Vacation . . . or Your Money Back!

As the owner of Perfect Place Travel, you're in charge of booking vacations. Naturally, you want your customers to have a great time. All of the people or groups listed below have come to you for advice. Where would you suggest each go on a vacation? Use each client's background to help you select the perfect place. Remember, your reputation is on the line!

1. Your first client is a rich, retired doctor who likes classical music, art, and museums. He does not like excitement, noise, or sports.

   Vacation spot recommended: _____

   Why? _____

2. Then you have a twenty-eight-year-old woman who is interested in history, ancient civilizations, old ruins, and photography.

   Vacation spot recommended: _____

   Why? _____

3. Next comes eight-year-old-twin boys, their ten-year-old sister, and their parents. The family loves nature, and doesn't want to spend a lot of money.

   Vacation spot recommended: _____

   Why? _____

4. Finally, you need to find a vacation location for a couple in their late forties. They enjoy sailing, night clubs, sightseeing, and plenty of excitement.

   Vacation spot recommended: _____

   Why? _____

Synthesizing

Synthesis is the process of combining ideas in a new way, thereby developing a creative product or idea. Synthesizing can also help us translate complicated concepts into easy-to-understand ideas. For example, when a fifth grader explains photosynthesis to a kindergartner, the older student must synthesize and restate the scientific concept using words and ideas that the younger child can understand. In the process, the older student reinforces his or her own knowledge of the topic.

Encourage students to work together on these activities and to share their reasoning. Consider having groups model the activities for the class, sharing their thoughts.

Weaving A Magic Yarn

Pull together all the strands of critical thinking with this enjoyable activity. Tell students they are all going to work together to create a cooperative story. Begin the tale by selecting one of the story starters on the following page (or by asking a student to come up with his or her own). After the first paragraph is on paper, pass the story from student to student. Each child, in turn, adds a new paragraph. Encourage students to read what is already written and to add a paragraph that seems to logically follow. When the story is complete, read it aloud to the class. They will no doubt delight in the wonderful tale they helped to create.

Variation: Divide students into groups of three to five. Have each group create a story by passing a paper from student to student—each, in turn, adds a new paragraph. Have the groups share their completed stories with the class.

On the following page are some super story starters!

Story Starters

Story Starter 1

"This can't be happening," I muttered to myself, rubbing the sleep from my eyes. I shook my little brother awake and dragged him to the window. He gazed in amazement at the sight of . . .

Story Starter 2

My parents chose an out-of-the-way vacation spot because we all wanted a break from the blaring horns and screeching tires of the city. The hills outside our window were beautiful, gentle green slopes dotted with sheep. The quiet beauty made it all the more shocking when . . .

Story Starter 3

"Fasten your seatbelts and prepare for an emergency landing," the pilot barked. Suddenly, the engines revved and the plane began its descent. I took a great gulp of air and gripped the armrests. The pilot skillfully landed the massive craft. The passengers jumped up and down, cheering and hugging one another. I knew my adventure had just begun, however, when I saw where we landed . . . .

Response Rally

Here's a fun way to help your students build synthesis skills. Pose the following questions one at a time, challenging students to write down as many possible answers for each question as they can. When you're done, discuss students' responses. Encourage students to explain their answers.

1. Imagine your mother said to you, "I am glad you had an egg with toast before you went to school this morning." She did not prepare your breakfast; she did not see you eat it. How did she know what you ate?

2. Plants native to one region are found all over the world. Why?

3. How are animals and plants similar? How are they different?

4. Which things do you wish had *never* been invented? Why?

5. Why are homes around the world different?

6. If you could invent anything in the world, what would it be and why?

7. Name some books in which animals speak like people.

8. If you could be any age at all, what age would you be and why?

9. Name as many hobbies as you can.

10. Imagine you had a time machine that could take you backward or forward in time. Where would you go and why?

Response Rally (cont.)

11. If you were a superhero, who would you be and why?

12. List as many uses for paper as you can imagine.

13. What one thing would you do to improve the world?

14. Why do people speak different languages?

15. Imagine your parents said to you, "We wish you would not go out to play so early in the morning." They did not see you leave or enter the house; they did not see you outside. How did they know you went outside?

16. What would the United States be like if there was no government?

17. Who is your favorite writer? Why?

18. Do you wish dinosaurs were still alive? Why or why not?

19. Which sport do you think is the best? Why?

20. What would the world be like if people didn't have to sleep?

What If?

This literature-based activity is sure to hone your students' critical-thinking skills. First choose a novel or short story that every child has read and isolate a key event. For example, in *Dear Mr. Henshaw* by Beverly Cleary, Leigh's decision to keep a diary is a key event. But what if Leigh had decided *not* to keep a diary? Alter a key event in the story you've selected and pose a similar question to the class. Then, have students work in groups or individually to brainstorm and write down events in the story that would not have happened or would have happened differently as a result of that key event being altered. When everyone is done, discuss students' responses. Encourage them to support their claims.

Tape It!

On the blackboard, make a list of the many things your class has read throughout the course of the year including stories, novels, poems, essays, historical writings, etc. Assign all students a partner and ask them to choose a piece of writing. (If the work is a short story or a novel, ask students to select their favorite scene from the work.) Tell students they will be using a tape recorder to prepare an oral interpretation of that piece of writing. Discuss with students the various ways they can make their interpretations unique and dramatic. Make them aware of the "tools" they have to work with including pitch, articulation, volume, pacing, expression, and sound effects. Then have students work with their partners to plan their interpretations. Give each pair a turn with the tape recorder. Finally, play all the interpretations for the class to enjoy. Which ones were particularly effective and why?

The Invention Convention

Invite students to create and build their own fantastic inventions! Direct each student to begin by deciding on the function or his or her invention. Then, have the children fashion their inventions from commonplace materials such as cardboard boxes, paper, string, cardboard tubes, and found objects. When all the students have completed their work, have them write brief descriptions of their inventions' purposes and functions. Then encourage each student to share his or her invention with the class. If you like, you can award certificates for the most practical, the best designed, and the wackiest inventions!

Name _____

Round and Round . . .

How many things can you think of that are round? They can be flat or 3-D. Draw them below. The first one has been done for you.

After you have drawn your objects, write a short story in which you mention as many of the objects as you possibly can.

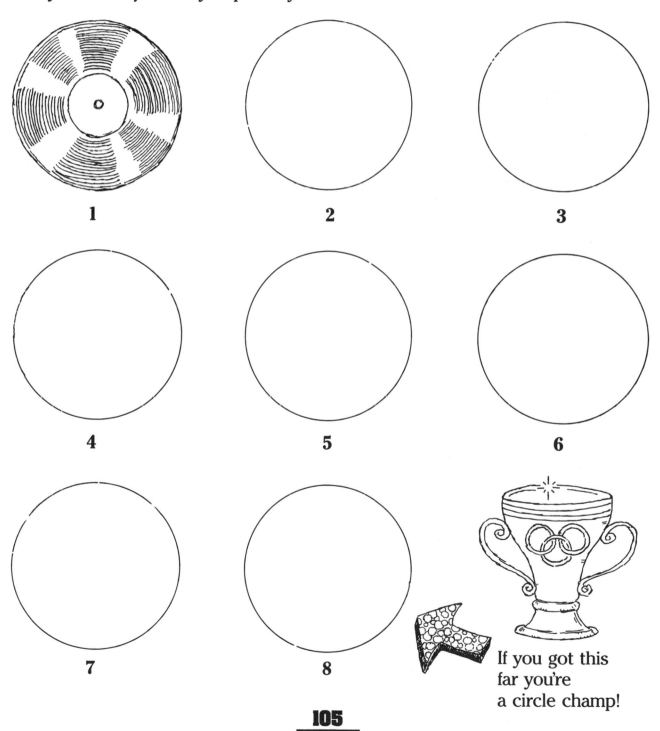

1

2

3

4

5

6

7

8

If you got this
far you're
a circle champ!

Name _____

Rainbow Creations

Think about a rainbow's special shape. Brainstorm a list of things that have a rainbow's arched shape such as a doorway, a tunnel, a horseshoe, and a boomerang. Now, think of some things that *should* have a rainbow's arched shape. Sketch your rainbow creations below. Be sure to include a description of each. When you're done, share your rainbow creations with a friend.

Create a rainbow-shaped home.

Create a rainbow-shaped food item.

Description: _____

_____

_____

Description: _____

_____

_____

Create a rainbow-shaped toy.

Create a rainbow-shaped tool.

Description: _____

_____

_____

Description: _____

_____

_____

Name _____

Build a Better Mousetrap

Even things that are well designed can stand to be better designed. For example, wouldn't it be nice if your lunch box had an alarm system that would keep cookie snatchers away? Or, your bike had wings so that you could fly over to a friend's house? Well here's your chance to make some changes for the better. Choose one of the items from list A and add as many practical and far-out features from list B—and your imagination—as you like. Draw a picture of your "super-object" in the box below. And don't forget to write a description of it.

A		B	
roller skates	eyeglasses	pockets	mirror
skateboard	bike	buzzer	parachute
book	bed	cd player	flashing lights
sneakers	lunch box	wings	motor

Super Object: _____

_____

_____

Name _____

Change the World!

There are many problems facing America today. Some of these include pollution, homelessness, and crime. What do *you* think is the biggest problem our country faces? How would you solve it?

America's worst problem today is _____

You have four tools: money, education, other people, and your imagination. Explain how you would use each to solve the problem.

Money: _____
_____
_____
_____

Education: _____
_____
_____
_____

Other people: _____
_____
_____
_____

Your imagination: _____
_____
_____
_____
_____
_____

Answer Key

Answers

Recognizing and Recalling
Trivia Trackdown, page 13
1. 64
2. Pluto
3. an elephant
4. the Kitty Hawk
5. Albany
6. teeth
7. Sandra Day O'Connor
8. the chicken
9. Dr. Seuss
10. one
11. John Adams
12. three
13. Kansas and Missouri
14. Casper
15. Erie, Ontario, Michigan, Huron, Superior
16. Leonardo da Vinci
17. water
18. six
19. four
20. two

Recycled Words 1, page 14
1. eye
2. land
3. new
4. road
5. run
6. ship
7. rain
8. snow
9. play
10. egg

Recycled Words 2, page 15
1. pop
2. house
3. cat
4. place
5. star
6. black
7. water
8. storm
9. line
10. door

What's My Letter? 1, page 19
List 1
1. hail
2. haiku
3. half
4. hamburger
5. hay fever
6. heart
7. hero
8. high
9. history
10. Holland

What's My Letter? 2, page 20
List 2
1. lamp
2. large
3. laugh
4. lazy
5. left
6. leave
7. lemon
8. leopard
9. library
10. little

Distinguishing and Visualizing
Real Estate, page 27
1. 2   2. 5   3. 2   4. 9   5. 1
6. 4   7. 3   8. 4

Alien Invasion, page 28

Twin Cat Bash, page 29
Single cats: row 1, first and third cat from left; row 3, first cat from left

Stargazing, page 31

Wrong Rhymes, page 33

1. swam
2. got
3. kicked
4. sign
5. side
6. fork
7. sing
8. peek
9. lake
10. creak
11. jump
12. fun
13. taste
14. spill
15. beet
16. dead
17. sock
18. ate
19. hike
20. drop

Triangle Challenge, page 36

Answer: 13 triangles

Classifying

Clean-Up Time!, page 48

1. A kitten is not a wild animal.
2. A tack is not a tool.
3. Track is the only sport that does not use a ball.
4. Melon does not have a pit.
5. Albany is not a state.
6. Rubies are not metal.
7. You cannot write with a ruler.
8. Drums are not a woodwind instrument.
9. Every word but *arrive* means to leave.
10. The horse is not a baby animal.
11. You cannot read a radio.
12. A foot is not a part of a face.

Inferring and Drawing Conclusions

Constant Confusion, page 67

1. Jackie
2. Jennifer
3. Jessica
4. Judith
5. Justina

Make a Wish, page 68

denomination	amount	total
pennies	6	6¢
nickels	6	30¢
dimes	2	20¢

Loopy Language, page 69

Idiomatic meaning:

1. outdo all others
2. broken
3. get some sleep
4. make peace
5. it is a loser
6. joking with you
7. get the upper hand
8. caught committing the crime
9. very crazy
10. relax
11. survive a bad situation
12. eat a lot
13. crane neck to see something
14. by the narrowest margin
15. chat

Evaluating

What does It Represent?, page 73

Possible responses:

a dove: peace; an eagle: America, strength, power, victory; the American flag: America, democracy; a red rose: love, passion; a fox: craftiness, slyness; an owl: wisdom; a wedding ring: marriage; a four-leaf clover: luck

Fact or Opinion?, page 75

1. opinion
2. fact
3. opinion
4. fact
5. fact
6. opinion
7. fact
8. fact
9. fact
10. fact
11. opinion
12. fact
13. fact
14. opinion
15. fact
16. opinion
17. fact
18. opinion
19. fact
20. fact

Analyzing

Transformations, page 85

1. 3
2. 2
3. 2
4. 6
5. 5
6. 2

The Magic Number Is . . . , page 86

Answer: 36

Amazing Analogies, page 88

Possible responses:

1. ocean
2. foot
3. square
4. dog
5. soil
6. Halloween
7. floors
8. snow
9. bunch
10. paints
11. watch
12. sour

Odd Couples, page 89

Possible responses:

1. both are the young of the species; both require care
2. both are machines that convert words into type; both need human operators
3. both are means of communication; both can entertain
4. both help the environment; both come out after rain
5. both are sources of energy; both can be dangerous
6. both use air; both entertain
7. both are times of hope and possibility; both are part of a cycle
8. both are odd numbers; both are prime
9. both live in the jungle; both are hunted
10. both are fruits; both are red

Divide and Conquer, page 95

1.

2.

3. Triangle cannot be divided into four equal pieces.

4.